Kinky Cupcakes

Kinky Cupcakes

Joanna Farrow

spruce

An Hachette UK Company
First published in Great Britain in 2010 by Spruce
a division of Octopus Publishing Group Ltd
Endeavour House, 189 Shaftesbury Avenue,
London, WC2H 8JY
www.octopusbooksusa.com

Distributed in the U.S. and Canada for
Octopus Books USA
c/- Hachette Book Group USA
237 Park Avenue
New York, NY 10017

ISBN 13: 978-1-84601-364-5
ISBN 10: 1-84601-364-X

A CIP catalog record for this book is available from
the British Library.

Printed and bound in China

10 9 8 7 6 5 4 3 2 1

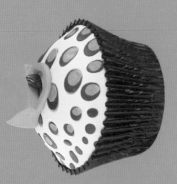

Contents

Introduction

The cupcake revolution has been gathering pace for some time now, capturing the imagination of cooks everywhere. Kinky Cupcakes comes at a good moment to provide an exciting, artistic, and creative new twist on the theme. Here is your chance to create a range of sexy, fun, quirky cakes that are perfect for a variety of occasions from birthdays to girls' nights, and from bachelorette parties to Valentine's Day. Or, on a more intimate level, you could use some of these cute and coquettish creations to entice your partner...

You might want to make a whole batch of one design, or mix and match a few of your favorite decorations within each batch of cakes. Some of the distinctive designs are simple to create but most require a little time, patience, and creative input to achieve

stylish, rewarding results. These are cakes to become engrossed in, enjoy, and nurture to your heart's content.

Buying supplies

A good cake decorating store will stock all the decorating ingredients and tools you can't buy in the supermarket. Otherwise, check out the Internet for mail-order suppliers.

Check through each recipe before you start. Some include decorations that require overnight setting before assembling, others might need a food coloring or cutter that you'll need to buy.

Choosing cupcake cups

In all the Kinky cake designs in this book, the cupcake cups are as much a part of the overall look as the decoration, and the right color or style will really help to set off the cakes. Most supermarkets sell only plain cupcake cups, but there are plenty of stunning designs available from other outlets. Bear in mind that they vary

considerably in size, ranging from cute little baby cups to giant muffin cups. The size of your cups will obviously determine the number of cakes you get out of each recipe.

Tips for making and storing cupcakes

As a guide, fill the cupcake cups no more than two-thirds full with cake mixture before baking, so the sponge has space to rise as it bakes. If under-filled they won't look effective, if over-filled the mixture will spill out as it cooks. Cook the cakes in the center of a preheated oven. If the cupcakes fill more than one tray, bake in two separate batches, rather than placing one tray at the top of the oven and the other at the bottom, then rotating the trays halfway through cooking. This will result in perfect cakes every time.

Cupcakes are best served freshly baked. If you don't have time to bake and decorate in the same session, keep the undecorated cakes in an airtight container for up to 24 hours. If storing for longer, it is better to freeze them, then thaw for several hours at room temperature before decorating.

Once decorated, store cupcakes in a cool place until you eat them, especially if they contain chocolate ganache. Don't put them in the refrigerator, however, or toppings such as ganache and cream cheese frosting will become too hard.

Basic Recipes

Vanilla Cupcakes

1 vanilla bean, or 2 teaspoons vanilla extract
1 cup superfine sugar
¼ cup (1 stick) lightly salted butter, softened
2 eggs
1 tablespoon milk
Scant 1¼ cups self-rising flour
(Makes 10)

1) Line 10 cups of a muffin pan with paper cupcake cups and preheat the oven to 350°F.

2) Split the vanilla bean lengthwise, if using, and scrape out the seeds with the tip of a knife. Put in a mixing bowl with a spoonful of the sugar and mash together until the seeds are evenly distributed. Add the remaining sugar and cake ingredients and beat with an electric beater until pale and creamy. Alternatively, simply beat the vanilla extract with the remaining ingredients.

3) Divide the mixture among the cupcake cups and bake in the oven for about 25 minutes until risen and just firm. Transfer to a cooling rack to cool.

Cherry Cupcakes

Make *Vanilla Cupcakes*, using 1 teaspoon of almond extract instead of the vanilla and ½ cup of ground almonds to replace ¼ cup of the flour. Stir in ½ cup of chopped candied cherries before baking.

Rich Chocolate Cupcakes

Scant 1 cup unsweetened cocoa powder
Scant 1 cup (7½ fl oz) boiling water
¼ lb (1 stick) lightly salted butter, softened
1¼ cups brown sugar
2 eggs
Generous 1½ cups all-purpose flour
2 teaspoons baking powder
(Makes 12)

1) Line 12 cups of a muffin pan with paper cupcake cups and preheat the oven to 350°F.

2) Put the cocoa powder in a bowl and beat in the measured boiling water. Leave to cool.

3) Beat together the butter and sugar until pale and creamy. Gradually beat in the eggs. Sift the flour and baking powder into the bowl and stir well. Once combined, add the cocoa mixture and stir again to mix well.

4) Divide the mixture among the cupcake cups and bake in the oven for about 25 minutes until risen and just firm. Leave in the tin for 10 minutes, then transfer to a cooling rack to cool.

Chocolate Chile Cupcakes

Make *Rich Chocolate Cupcakes*, beating 1 teaspoon of crushed dried chiles with the butter and sugar.

Chocolate Rose Cupcakes

Make *Rich Chocolate Cupcakes*, adding 2 tablespoons of rosewater with the eggs.

Tutti Frutti Cupcakes

Scant ½ cup (3½ fl oz) fruit liqueur (Cointreau,
    Grand Marnier, Apricot, or Cherry Brandy)
¾ cup dried strawberries
¾ cup dried blueberries
¼ lb (1 stick) lightly salted butter, softened
1 cup superfine sugar
2 eggs
Scant 1¼ cups self-rising flour
Scant ½ cup pistachio nuts, chopped
(Makes 10)

1) Line 10 cups of a muffin pan with paper
    cupcake cups and preheat the oven to
    350°F.

2) Put the liqueur in a measuring jug and add
    the dried fruits. Use a fork to pierce the fruits.
    This will help the liqueur to be absorbed.

3) Put the butter, sugar, eggs, and flour in a
    bowl and beat with an electric beater until
    pale and creamy.

4) Drain the unabsorbed liqueur into the bowl
    and stir well. Add the fruits and nuts and stir
    until evenly combined.

5) Divide the mixture among the cupcake cups
    and bake in the oven for about 25 minutes
    until risen and just firm. Transfer to a cooling
    rack to cool.

Exotic Spice Cupcakes

1 lemongrass stalk
Generous ¾ cup superfine sugar
12 cardamom pods
2½ lb (⅝ stick) lightly salted butter, softened
2 eggs
2 oz fresh root ginger, peeled and
    finely grated
Generous 1½ cups all-purpose flour
2 teaspoons baking powder
Scant ½ cup (3½ fl oz) milk
Scant 1 cup dried mango, chopped
(Makes 10)

1) Line 10 cups of a muffin pan with paper
    cupcake cups and preheat the oven to
    375°F.

2) Remove the coarse outer leaves from the
    lemongrass, trim off the ends, and chop the
    core as finely as possible. Whizz in a food

processor with the sugar. Crush the cardamom pods using a mortar and pestle, discard the shells, and crush the seeds a little more.

3) Put all the ingredients, except the mango, in a mixing bowl and beat with an electric beater until smooth and creamy. Stir in the mango.

4) Divide the mixture among the cupcake cups and bake in the oven for about 20 minutes until risen and just firm. Transfer to a cooling rack to cool.

Red Velvet Cupcakes

Generous 1½ cups self-rising flour
2 tablespoons unsweetened cocoa powder
½ teaspoon baking soda
⅔ cup (7fl oz) buttermilk
1 teaspoon vinegar
1 teaspoon vanilla extract
3½ oz (⅞ stick) lightly salted butter, softened
1 cup superfine sugar
2 eggs
3½ oz raw beets, finely grated
(Makes 10)

1) Line 10 cups of a muffin pan with paper cupcake cups and preheat the oven to 350°F.

2) Combine the flour, cocoa powder, and baking soda in a bowl. Mix together the buttermilk, vinegar, and vanilla in a jug.

3) In a large mixing bowl, beat together the butter and sugar until pale and creamy, then beat in the eggs, grated beets, and 4 tablespoons of the flour mixture to prevent curdling.

4) Sift half the remaining flour mixture into the bowl and fold in gently with a large metal spoon. Stir in the buttermilk mixture, then sift and fold in the remaining flour until just combined.

5) Divide the mixture among the cupcake cups and bake in the oven for about 25 minutes until risen and just firm. Transfer to a cooling rack to cool.

Buttercream

3½ oz (¾ stick) unsalted butter, softened
1¾ cups confectioners' sugar
(Makes 8 oz)

1) Put the butter and confectioners' sugar in a
bowl and beat well with an electric beater
until pale and creamy.

Vodka Buttercream

Make the basic Buttercream, then gradually
beat in 5 tablespoons of vodka until the
mixture is smooth.

Amaretto Buttercream

Make the basic Buttercream, then gradually
beat in 5 tablespoons of almond liqueur until
the mixture is smooth.

Cream Cheese Frosting

Generous 1 cup cream cheese
½ teaspoon vanilla extract
1¼ cups confectioners' sugar
(Makes 11½ oz)

1) Put all the ingredients in a mixing bowl and
beat together until smooth and creamy. Chill
for 1 hour until the frosting has thickened a
little, then spread or pipe over the cakes.

Coconut Frosting

5 tablespoons light cream
¼ cup coconut cream, chopped if firm
1 tablespoon lime juice
2½ cups confectioners' sugar
(Makes 13 oz)

1) Put the light cream and coconut cream in
a small saucepan and heat gently until the
coconut has melted. Pour into a mixing bowl

with the lime juice and confectioners' sugar and beat with an electric beater until the mixture is thick and smooth. Spread or pipe over the cakes.

Dark Chocolate Ganache

1¼ cups (10 fl oz) heavy cream
10 oz semisweet chocolate, chopped
(Makes 1 lb 3 oz)

1) Heat the cream in a small saucepan until almost boiling. Pour into a bowl and stir in the chocolate. Leave for a few minutes, stirring frequently, until the chocolate has melted.

2) Leave to cool completely, then chill until the mixture has thickened enough to spread over the cakes. If you are using the ganache for piping, beat it lightly with an electric beater to thicken it further.

White Chocolate Ganache

1¼ cups (10 fl oz) heavy cream
10 oz white chocolate, chopped
(Makes 1 lb 3 oz)

1) Heat half the cream in a small saucepan until almost boiling. Pour into a bowl and stir in the chocolate. Leave for a few minutes, stirring frequently, until the chocolate has melted.

2) Leave to cool completely, then stir in the remaining cream and beat with an electric beater until the ganache just holds its shape. Don't over-beat or the texture might spoil.

Decorating Techniques

Using food colorings

Gel food colorings give deep shades. Dot rolled fondant with the gel using the tip of a cocktail stick. Knead the fondant on a surface dusted with confectioner's sugar until the color is evenly distributed. For royal icing, beat small amounts of gel in until you reach the right shade.

Liquid food colorings generally give less intense colors, but are good for pastel shades and for painting onto icing.

Powder colorings produce intense shades and can be mixed into icings in the same way as gels. They are also good for dusting.

Metallic colorings, such as gold and silver, can be bought in liquid form (stir well before use) or as a powder, which can be mixed with a flavorless oil or a dash of vodka so it can be used for painting on. Check colors are edible; if not, remove the decorated area before serving.

As with artists' paints, the best shades are made by mixing basic colors. If you have a limited palette, mix different proportions of red and blue to create lilac, burgundy, and purple. Blend red and yellow to make orange. Chestnut brown paste is good for flesh tones, or mix a dash of pink with dark brown.

Making a paper piping bag

Paper piping bags are useful as they're easy to make, disposable after use, and don't necessarily require a decorating tip for piping fine lines. The amount you snip off the tip will determine the thickness of the line of icing, so only snip off a tiny amount at a time. For a more professional finish, fit with a fine decorating tip.

To make a bag, cut a 10 inch square of baking parchment and cut it in half to make two triangles. Place one triangle with the long edge away from you. Curl the right-hand point over and down to meet the lower, center point. The back of the right-hand point should meet the front of the lower point to form a cone. Now bring the left-hand point over and round the back of the cone so that the three points meet. You may need to slide the points around to get a tightly closed tip. Fold the points over several times to stop the cone unraveling. Snip off a tiny bit of the bag tip, or cut off a bigger piece and insert a decorating tip, if using. Half-fill the bag with icing and twist the top to close.

Making royal icing decorations

Royal icing decorations, such as the kinky boots (see page 92), are made and set on baking parchment. Pipe the shape outlines first using a paper piping bag with a tiny hole in it; make sure there are no gaps in the piping. Then thin the remaining icing with a little water and put it in another piping bag with a slightly larger hole. Use to fill in the shapes, easing the icing into any corners with the tip of a cocktail stick. Leave to harden for about 24 hours before removing the shapes from the paper.

Making icing ruffles

To make icing ruffles, roll out a long strip of rolled fondant on a surface dusted with confectioner's sugar. Roll the end of a cocktail stick along one side of the strip so it becomes

ruffled. Lift from the surface and re-dust with confectioner's sugar so the ruffle doesn't stick, then roll with the cocktail stick again. The more you roll the cocktail stick over the icing, the more ruffled the edge will become. Trim the unruffled edge of the strip, to leave a straight edge. Carefully lift the ruffle and position on the cupcake. Once on the cake, ruffles can be lifted and folded with the tip of a cocktail stick.

Melting chocolate

To melt on a stove top, chop the chocolate into small pieces, and put in a heatproof bowl. Rest the bowl over a pan of very gently simmering water, making sure the base doesn't touch the water. Once the chocolate starts to melt, turn off the heat and leave until completely melted, stirring once or twice. No water or steam from the pan should seep into the bowl while the chocolate is melting or it will solidify.

To melt in a microwave, chop the chocolate into small pieces and put in a microwave-safe bowl. Melt in one-minute bursts, checking frequently. Take care, particularly when melting white or sweet chocolate, as they have higher sugar contents and are more prone to scorching.

Maneater

9 oz semisweet chocolate, chopped * 1 quantity White Chocolate Ganache (see page 13)
* 12 Rich Chocolate Cupcakes (see page 9) * 12 small pink bows (optional) * Makes 12

One: Trace the outline of a female figure onto a piece of baking parchment. It should be roughly 3½ inches from head to toe. For guidance use the photograph opposite, or refer to a book or the Internet to source your image.

Two: Melt the chocolate (see page 15) and put it in a paper piping bag (see page 14). Snip off the merest tip of the bag. Place another sheet of parchment over the female outline. Pipe chocolate around the edges of the shape and then fill in the middle with more chocolate. Slide the top sheet of parchment along so you can pipe more figures. Leave to set.

Three: Spread the ganache over the cooled cupcakes. Carefully peel away the paper from the chocolate shapes and gently push them into the ganache. Decorate the cupcake cups with pink bows, if liked.

Frill Me!

10 Vanilla Cupcakes (see page 8) ✳ 1 quantity Vodka Buttercream (see page 12)
✳ 11 oz black rolled fondant ✳ 8 oz white rolled fondant ✳ Confectioners' sugar, for dusting
✳ Makes 10

One: Use a metal spatula to spread the cooled cupcakes with the buttercream.

Two: Dust a work surface with confectioners' sugar and roll out 3½ oz of the black fondant until ¼ inch thick. Cut out 10 hearts using a small round cutter. Place on a baking tray lined with baking parchment. Use a thick skewer to impress holes around the edges of the hearts, then leave for several hours to harden.

Three: Roll out a further 1 oz of the black fondant into a strip about ⅞ inch wide. Ruffle one edge of the strip (see page 15). Lay the ruffled strip around the edges of one cupcake, pleating it at intervals to give volume, and trimming off the excess where the ends join. Use the remaining icing and trimmings and roll more strips to cover the edges of the remaining cakes in the same way.

Four: On a clean surface, use the white fondant to create more ruffled strips in the same way and arrange on the cakes, just inside the black ruffles. Repeat, layering the ruffles and finishing with the white. Rest a black heart in the center of each cake to finish.

Take a Bow

4 egg whites ✻ Generous 1½ cup confectioners' sugar, plus extra for dusting ✻ ½ teaspoon cream of tartar ✻ Pinch of salt ✻ Deep pink food coloring ✻ 10 Red Velvet Cupcakes (see page 11) ✻ 2 oz black rolled fondant ✻ Makes 10

One: Put the egg whites, confectioners' sugar, cream of tartar, salt, and a dash of pink food coloring in a heatproof bowl. Rest the bowl over a pan of gently simmering water, making sure the base of the bowl doesn't touch the water. Beat using a hand-held electric beater for about 5 minutes until the frosting starts to thicken.

Two: Check the color of the frosting. If it is too pale, beat in a little more coloring to make a rich, deep shade of pink. Remove from the heat and beat for a further 5 minutes, or until it forms a softly peaking meringue-like mixture.

Three: Pile the frosting onto the cooled cupcakes and create peaks with a metal spatula or the back of a spoon.

Four: Dust a work surface with confectioners' sugar and roll out the black fondant thinly. Cut into ¾ x ¼ inch rectangles. Pinch the rectangles together in the centers with the tines of two forks to create simple bows. Arrange several bows on each cupcake.

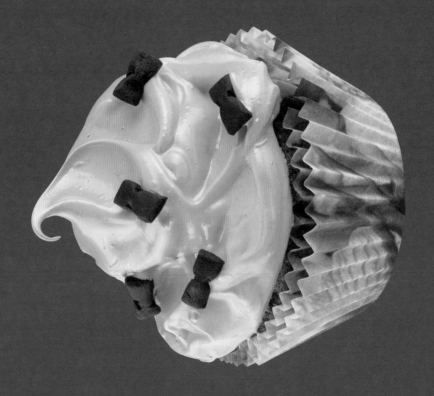

Hunk a' Love

12 Rich Chocolate Cupcakes (see page 9) ✹ 2 cups chocolate hazelnut spread ✹ 1 lb flesh-colored rolled fondant ✹ 3½ oz white rolled fondant ✹ Brown food coloring ✹ 2 oz burgundy rolled fondant ✹ 1½ oz black rolled fondant ✹ Confectioners' sugar, for dusting ✹ Makes 12

One: Use a metal spatula to spread one half of each cooled cupcake with the chocolate spread.

Two: Dust a work surface with confectioners' sugar. Take a 1½ oz piece of flesh-colored fondant and flatten it to about the same diameter as a cake top. Use your fingers to impress chest markings onto the surface. Position on one of the cakes, propping it up on the chocolate spread at the back. Make the remainder in the same way.

Three: Thinly roll out the white fondant and cut into thin strips. Position a strip on each side of each chest to resemble an opened shirt. Secure in place with a dampened paintbrush and add buttonholes on one side.

Four: Use a little diluted brown food coloring and a fine paintbrush to paint chest contours and nipples.

Five: Thinly roll out the burgundy fondant and cut into long thin strips. Arrange on the cupcakes to resemble long ties. Use the black fondant to make three buttons for each cake. Make the holes with a cocktail stick and arrange on the shirts.

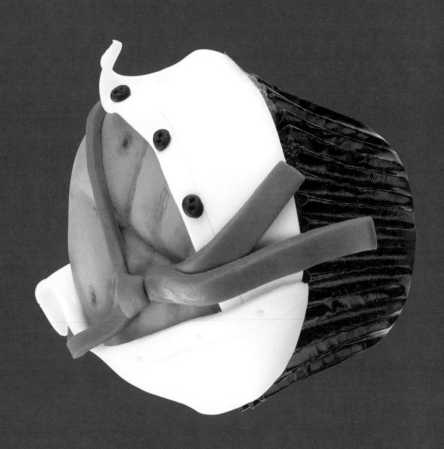

Dominatrix Delights

3½ oz white rolled fondant ✱ 1 quantity Cream Cheese Frosting (see page 12) ✱ Pink food coloring ✱ 10 Vanilla Cupcakes (see page 8) ✱ 3½ oz black rolled fondant ✱ Edible silver food coloring ✱ Confectioners' sugar, for dusting ✱ Makes 10

One: Dust a work surface with confectioners' sugar and thinly roll out the white fondant. Cut out 2 small rings for each cake and place on a baking tray lined with baking parchment. This can be done with 2 small round cutters, one ¾ inch and one ⅞ inch in diameter. Cut out 2 tiny rectangles for each cake to finish the handcuffs, and secure to the rings with a dampened paintbrush.

Two: Reroll the trimmings and cut out 10 keys using a small sharp knife. Roll tiny balls of fondant and flatten slightly for chains. You'll need 3 for each cake. Leave to harden for at least 2 hours.

Three: Color the frosting with pink food coloring and use a metal spatula to smooth it over the tops of the cooled cupcakes.

Four: Roll out the black fondant and cut into very thin strips, about ⅛ inch. Drape over the cakes, letting some loops overhang the edges. To make the tassels, cut out ¾ x ½ inch rectangles. Score through the rectangles, keeping one long edge intact. Dampen the long edge and roll up. Secure to the ends of the black strips by using a dampened paintbrush and pinching them in place.

Five: Use the silver food coloring to paint the handcuffs and keys and allow to dry. Arrange on top of the cupcakes.

Sealed with a Kiss

3½ oz deep red rolled fondant ✳ 7 oz white rolled fondant ✳ 10 Red Velvet Cupcakes (see page 11)
✳ ½ quantity Vodka Buttercream (see page 12) ✳ 8 oz ivory rolled fondant ✳ Edible gold food
coloring ✳ Edible confectioners' glaze ✳ Red food coloring ✳ Confectioners' sugar, for dusting
✳ Makes 10

One: Dust a work surface with confectioners' sugar and roll out the red fondant under the palms of your hands to a log shape about ¾ inch thick. Cut into 10 lengths, each about 1¼ inches long, making every other cut diagonal to form the points of the lipsticks.

Two: Roll out the white fondant to a slightly thicker log and cut into 20 lengths, 10 at 1¾ inches and 10 at 1¼ inches long. Use a dampened paintbrush to secure the red pieces to the longer white pieces. Transfer all the pieces to a baking tray lined with baking parchment and leave to harden overnight.

Three: Use a metal spatula to spread the cooled cupcakes with the buttercream, doming it up slightly in the centers. Thinly roll out the ivory fondant and cut out 10 discs using a 3½ inch round cutter. Arrange over the cupcakes, smoothing down gently.

Four: Use a fine paintbrush to paint the white parts of the lipsticks with gold food coloring. Leave to dry, then paint the red and gold parts with confectioners' glaze.

Five: When dry, secure the lipsticks to the cupcakes with a dampened paintbrush. Finish by using a fine paintbrush and red food coloring to paint lips to one side of each lipstick.

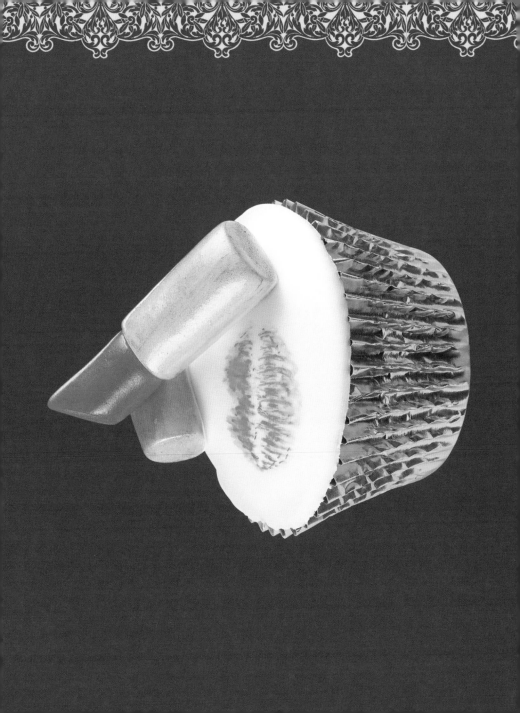

Hella Sailor!

½ quantity Dark Chocolate Ganache (see page 13) ✳ *12 Rich Chocolate Cupcakes (see page 9)* ✳ *8 oz flesh-colored rolled fondant* ✳ *Black and red food colorings* ✳ *Confectioners' sugar, for dusting* ✳ **Makes 12**

One: Use a metal spatula to spread the ganache on the cooled cupcakes.

Two: Dust a work surface with confectioners' sugar, roll out the flesh-colored fondant thinly and cut out 12 discs using a 3½ inch cutter. Place one disc on each cupcake, smoothing down to eliminate any creases. Leave for several hours or overnight to harden.

Three: Use the food colorings and a fine paintbrush to paint tattoo designs on the icing discs, choosing your own design or copying the one in the photograph.

Dark Angel

13 oz black rolled fondant ✻ 1 oz red rolled fondant ✻ Generous 1½ cups royal icing sugar ✻ Black food coloring ✻ 1 quantity Coconut Frosting (see page 12) ✻ 10 Vanilla Cupcakes (see page 8) ✻ Confectioners' sugar, for dusting ✻ 12 ft ribbon ✻ Makes 10

One: Divide the black fondant into 10 equal pieces and cut each piece in half. Dust your hands with confectioners' sugar and mold each piece into a wing, 10 left and 10 right, each about 1¾ inches deep and 2½ inches wide. Press 2 wings together to form a pair, securing with a dampened paintbrush. Place on a baking tray lined with baking parchment.

Two: Dust a work surface with confectioners' sugar and roll out the red fondant. Cut out tiny hearts using a ½ inch cutter. Transfer to the baking tray.

Three: Put the royal icing sugar in a bowl and add enough water, about 5 teaspoons, to mix to a smooth paste. Beat in the black food coloring. Put the icing in a paper piping bag (see page 14) and snip off the merest tip. Use to pipe a lacy design all over the wings. Position a red heart in the center of each. Leave for several hours or overnight to harden.

Four: Use a metal spatula to spread the frosting over the tops of the cooled cupcakes. Carefully position a set of wings on each cake.

Five: Cut a 12 inch length of ribbon and tie around each cupcake cup to decorate. You might need to apply a dot of glue around the back to hold the ribbon in place.

Temptation

11 oz White almond paste ✳ Purple and dark green food colorings ✳ 5 oz pale green rolled fondant
✳ 1 quantity Amaretto Buttercream (see page 12) ✳ 10 Cherry Cupcakes (see page 8)
✳ Confectioners' sugar, for dusting ✳ Makes 10

One: Divide the almond paste into 10 equal pieces. Dust your hands with confectioners' sugar, roll each piece into a ball, and pinch out a point on one side. Cut off the tip of the point. Paint the tips of the figs green and the rest purple. For the most effective results, refer to a photograph of a fig to get the colors just right.

Two: Dust a work surface with confectioners' sugar and roll out the green fondant as thinly as possible. Cut out fig leaves using cutters in two or three sizes. If you can't get fig leaf cutters, use an ivy cutter. Mark veins on the leaves with the tip of a knife. Twist into natural shapes and transfer to a sheet of crumpled foil. Leave for several hours or overnight to harden.

Three: Once the leaves are hard, paint them with dark green food coloring.

Four: Use a metal spatula to spread the buttercream over the cooled cupcakes and gently press the figs on top. Arrange the leaves around the figs, resting them on the buttercream and securing onto the figs with dots of buttercream.

Devilishly Good

1 quantity Dark Chocolate Ganache (see page 13) ✳ 12 Chocolate Chile Cupcakes (see page 9) ✳ 24 small fresh red chiles ✳ Edible red dusting powder ✳ 8¼ ft feather boa ✳ Makes 12

One Put the chocolate ganache in a large paper piping bag (see page 14) fitted with a large star nozzle. Pipe a lavish swirl of ganache on top of each cooled cupcake and position 2 small red chiles on top.

Two Use your fingers to sprinkle a little red dusting powder over each cupcake. Cut 12 lengths out of the feather boa, then wrap a length round each cupcake cup, holding it in place with a little glue.

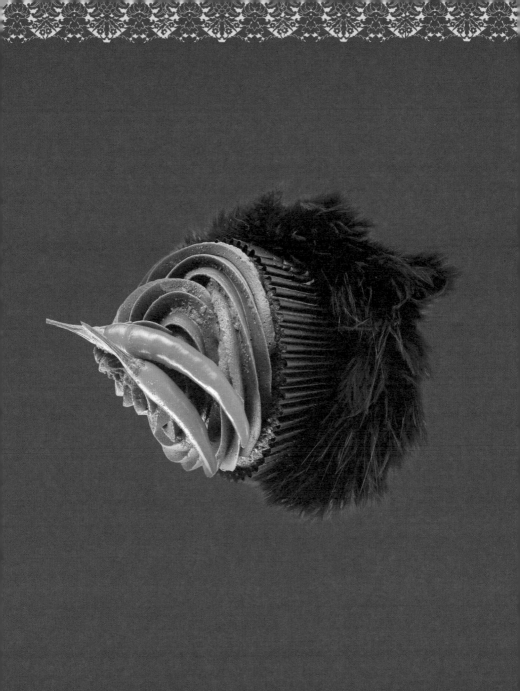

Thorny Passion

1 quantity *Coconut Frosting* (see page 12) ❋ 10 *Red Velvet Cupcakes* (see page 11)
❋ 1 lb 6 oz deep red rolled fondant ❋ *Clear piping gel* (optional) ❋ *Confectioners' sugar,
for dusting* ❋ Makes 10

One: Use a metal spatula to spread the frosting over the cupcakes. Divide the red fondant into 10 equal pieces.

Two: Take one piece of fondant and wrap the other pieces tightly in plastic wrap. Dust your hands with confectioners' sugar, break off a grape-sized piece and shape it into a cone, pressing the thick end down on a work surface. Pinch the cone in near the base to form a "waist".

Three: Take a small ball of fondant and shape it into a petal, pressing it as thin as possible until it is about 1¼ inches in diameter. The finer the petals are, the more realistic the rose will be. Wrap the petal around the cone so it curls tightly around the top to form the center of the rose.

Four: Shape another slightly larger petal and wrap around the cone on the opposite side. Continue layering the petals, making each slightly larger than the one before and opening them out as you work away from the center. Roll over the top edges of the outer petals for a realistic effect.

Five: Using a sharp knife, slice the rose off the work surface and transfer to one of the cupcakes, then make the remainder in the same way. Put a spoonful of piping gel in a paper piping bag (see page 14) and snip off the tip. Pipe drops of gel onto the rose petals for a rain drop effect, if liked.

Frills and Thrills

8 oz flesh-colored rolled fondant ✳ 3½ oz black rolled fondant ✳ 1 quantity White Chocolate Ganache (see page 13) ✳ Turquoise food coloring ✳ 10 Tutti Frutti Cupcakes (see page 10) ✳ 10 ft black beading ✳ Confectioners' sugar, for dusting ✳ **Makes 10**

One: Divide the flesh-colored fondant into 10 equal pieces, dust your hands with confectioners' sugar and shape each piece into a bottom with thighs and waist. Place the bottoms on a baking tray lined with baking parchment.

Two: Dust a work surface with confectioners' sugar, roll out the black fondant thinly, and cut out 10 skimpy bikinis. Secure onto the bottoms using a dampened paintbrush.

Three: Reroll the black fondant trimmings and cut a strip about ¼ inch wide. Ruffle one edge of the strip (see page 15). Trim off the unfrilled edge and secure the frill to the bikinis, cutting off the excess at the sides. Repeat to make 2 frills on each pair of bikinis.

Four: Color the ganache with turquoise food coloring, then spread over the tops of the cooled cupcakes with a metal spatula. Position the decorations on top and tie strings of beads around the sides of the cupcake cups, securing with a little glue at the back, if necessary.

Wandering Hands

1½ oz black rolled fondant ❊ edible confectioner's glaze ❊ 3½ oz lilac rolled fondant
❊ 10 Exotic Spice Cupcakes (see page 10) ❊ 1 quantity Cream Cheese Frosting (see page 12)
❊ Confectioners' sugar, for dusting ❊ Makes 10

One: Take a 1 oz piece of black fondant and cut in half. Dust your hands with confectioners' sugar, then shape each piece into a hand, 10 left and 10 right. The easiest way is to make a roll about 2 inches long with a mitten shape at the end. Make 4 cuts with the tip of a sharp knife to shape fingers and thumb, then roll the fingers slightly to smooth out the cut edges. Place the hands in pairs on a baking tray lined with baking parchment, then bend them back at the wrists. Paint the hands with edible confectioners' glaze and leave them to dry.

Two: Cut the lilac fondant into 10 equal pieces, then shape each into a perfume bottle with a lid. Sit the bottles in the palms of the hands. Push a wooden cocktail stick up through the base of each hand and into the bottle, leaving a little of the stick protruding at each wrist. Leave to harden for several hours or overnight.

Three: Spread the cooled cupcakes with the frosting. Carefully lift the hands from the paper and press the sticks down gently into the cakes.

Four: Use the remaining black fondant to make the roses. Take a pea-sized piece of black fondant and roll it under your fingers until about 2 inches long. Press flat so until it about ¼ inch wide, then roll up to resemble a simple rose shape. Press gently into the frosting around the top edges of the cupcakes.

Burlesque Bites

1 vanilla bean ✳ 1 quantity Vodka Buttercream (see page 12) ✳ 10 Vanilla Cupcakes (see page 8) ✳ 3 oz black rolled fondant ✳ Tube of black writing icing ✳ Edible gold food coloring ✳ 10 ft fine ribbon ✳ Confectioners' sugar, for dusting ✳ Makes 10

One: Split the vanilla bean lengthwise with the tip of a sharp knife. Scrape out the seeds and mix in a bowl with a tablespoon of the buttercream to distribute the seeds evenly. Beat in the remaining buttercream and spread over the cooled cupcakes with a metal spatula.

Two: Dust your hands with confectioners' sugar. Take ⅓ oz of black fondant and mold it into the shape of a basque. Dust a work surface with confectioners' sugar, then thinly roll out a little more of the black fondant into a strip about ¼ inch wide. Ruffle one edge of the strip (see page 15). Dampen the unfilled edge with a paintbrush. Secure a frill to both top and bottom edges of the basque, trimming off any excess.

Three: Position the basque on one of the cupcakes, then make the remainder in the same way. Pipe a row of buttons down the center of each basque using the black writing icing. Paint the buttons with gold food coloring.

Four: Cut a 12-inch length of ribbon and tie around each cupcake cup to decorate. You might need to apply a dot of glue around the back to hold the ribbon in place.

Je t'aime

3½ oz each of white, lilac, and pink rolled fondant ✳ Tube of white writing icing ✳ Red and black food colorings ✳ 10 Vanilla Cupcakes (see page 8) ✳ 1 quantity of White Chocolate Ganache (see page 13) ✳ Confectioners' sugar, for dusting ✳ Makes 10

One Dust a work surface with confectioners' sugar and roll out the white fondant to ⅛ inch thick. Cut out discs using a 1¼ inch round cutter. Transfer to a baking tray lined with baking parchment and reroll the trimmings to make more discs. Repeat with the lilac and pink fondants. Leave to harden for at least 2 hours or overnight.

Two Use the white writing icing to pipe a heart onto each disc. Use red and black food colorings and a fine paintbrush to decorate the discs with little hearts or messages, and leave to dry.

Three Use a metal spatula to spread the cupcakes with the chocolate ganache. Arrange the fondant discs on the cooled cupcakes, securing in place with the writing icing left in the tube.

44

Heaven Scent

1 quantity White Chocolate Ganache (see page 13) ✳ 12 Chocolate Rose Cupcakes (see page 9) ✳ 4 oz black rolled fondant ✳ 4 oz white rolled fondant ✳ 4 oz ivory rolled fondant ✳ Edible pearlized pink dusting powder ✳ Edible silver food coloring ✳ Large silver shapes ✳ Confectioners' sugar, for dusting ✳ Makes 12

One: Place the ganache in a paper piping bag (see page 14) fitted with a star decorating tip, and pipe over the tops of the cooled cupcakes.

Two: Reserve ½ oz of the black fondant. Dust a work surface with confectioners' sugar and roll the remaining black fondant into a rope about 20 inches long. Roll the white fondant to the same length, then roll it with the black rope until the two hold together. Fold the rope in half and roll again into a 20 inch rope. Repeat two or three times until the fondant is streaked black and white. Finally, roll the fondant into a 24 inch rope and cut into 12 equal pieces.

Three: Flatten each piece slightly and shape into a female form, narrowing in the center, pinching out breasts, and extending the shoulders slightly. Push one gently onto each cupcake. Shape the reserved black fondant into little stoppers and secure them with a dampened paintbrush.

Four: Thinly roll out the ivory fondant and cut into ½ inch strips. Dust both sides with pink dusting powder. Drape the strips, ribbon like, around the cupcakes and leave to harden.

Five: Use a fine paintbrush to paint the tops of the stoppers with silver food coloring. Tuck several silver balls in place, pushing them gently into the ganache.

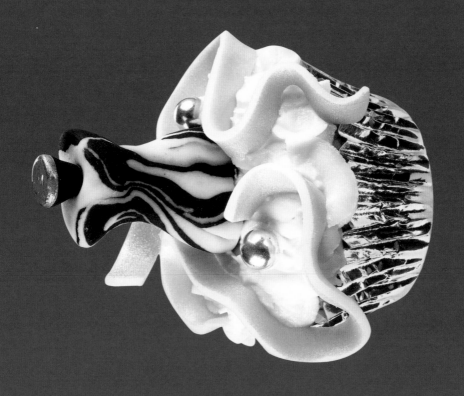

Fallen Angel

10 Vanilla Cupcakes (see page 8) * 1 quantity Coconut Frosting (see page 12)
* 4 tablespoons superfine sugar * Edible red glitter * 10 birthday cake candles * Vegetable oil,
for brushing * Makes 10

One: Use a metal spatula to spread the cooled cupcakes with coconut frosting.

Two: Line a large baking tray with a double thickness of kitchen paper, then completely cover the baking tray with foil. Lightly press a 2–2½ inch heart-shaped cutter onto the foil. The paper underneath the foil will help create an impression of the shape. Press 11 more hearts onto the foil. Brush the hearts lightly with vegetable oil.

Three: Sprinkle about a teaspoon of sugar into each heart shape, defining the edges well but thinning out the sugar in the center of each heart. Place the baking tray under a preheated hot grill and cook, watching closely, for a few minutes until most of the sugar has melted to a very pale caramel but some sugar crystals remain. Leave to cool.

Four: Carefully peel away the foil from the hearts, then sprinkle a fine trail of glitter around the edges of each. Press the hearts down gently into the frosting and sprinkle a little more dusting powder on the cupcakes. Position a candle behind each heart, ready for lighting.

48

Blind Ambition

10 Tutti Frutti cupcakes (see page 10) ✻ 7 tablespoons strawberry jelly ✻ 4 egg whites

✻ Pink food colouring ✻ 1 cup superfine sugar ✻ Silver dragees ✻ Edible silver leaf

✻ Makes 10

One: Use a teaspoon to scoop out a small cavity from the center of each cupcake and spoon in the jelly. Preheat the oven to 425°F.

Two: Beat the egg whites with plenty of food coloring until softly peaking. Gradually add the sugar, a tablespoonful at a time, beating between each addition until the meringue is thick and glossy. Put half the meringue in a large paper piping bag (see page 14) fitted with a ½ inch plain decorating tip and pipe deep swirls of meringue onto half the cupcakes, finishing with a point on top of each. Keep the meringue inside the paper cups as it will expand slightly during baking. Repeat with the remainder.

Three: Gently press the silver dragees into the meringue at regular intervals. Bake in the preheated oven for 8–10 minutes until the meringue is just beginning to color. Leave to cool.

Four: Decorate the meringue with silver leaf. Tear off small pieces of leaf with tweezers and lay them on the meringue, then gently flatten out with a soft paintbrush.

Forbidden Fruits

10 oz red rolled fondant ✱ 10 cloves ✱ Red and brown food colorings ✱ Edible confectioners' glaze ✱ 10 Tutti Frutti Cupcakes (see page 10) ✱ 1 quantity Cream Cheese Frosting (see page 12) ✱ 5 oz dark orange rolled fondant ✱ Confectioners' sugar, for dusting ✱ **Makes 10**

One: Divide the red fondant into 10 equal pieces, dust a work surface with confectioners' sugar and roll each piece into a ball. Flatten the tops slightly and push a clove into each to resemble an apple stalk. Use the food colorings to paint darker areas on the apples, place on a baking tray lined with baking parchment, and brush with the confectioners' glaze. Allow to dry.

Two: Use a metal spatula to spread the cooled cupcakes with the cream cheese frosting. Position an apple on top of each cake.

Three: Divide the orange fondant into 10 equal pieces and roll each one under the palm of your hand to shape a snake. Make one end thicker than the other, flattening it slightly into a head, and tapering the thin end to a point. Each snake should be about 9 inches long.

Four: Coil the snakes around the apples, letting the tails hang over the sides of the cupcake cups. Use the food colorings and a fine paintbrush to paint the details on the snakes.

Dressed to Kill

8 oz red rolled fondant ✳ 8 oz brandy-flavored almond paste ✳ 10 Cherry Cupcakes (see page 8)
✳ 2 cups confectioners' sugar, plus extra for dusting ✳ Black food coloring ✳ **Makes 10**

One: Take ¾ oz of red fondant and divide equally in half. Dust your hands with confectioners' sugar and mold the pieces of fondant into a pair of shoes, either copying the photograph opposite or using a design of your choice. Transfer to a baking tray lined with baking parchment and leave to harden while shaping the remainder.

Two: Cut the almond paste into 10 even-sized pieces and flatten into small, slightly domed discs, about 2 inches in diameter. Position a disc on the center of each cooled cupcake.

Three: Put the confectioners' sugar in a small bowl and stir in enough water, about 6–7 teaspoons, to make a smooth paste that thickly coats the back of the spoon. Spread over the cupcakes to cover the almond paste and run almost to the edges of the cakes.

Four: Position a pair of shoes on each cake, then use a fine paintbrush to decorate the shoes with black food coloring.

Girl's Best Friend

* 6 clear hard candy
* 4 oz ivory rolled fondant
* 10 Red Velvet Cupcakes (see page 11)
* ½ quantity Cream Cheese Frosting (see page 12)
* 10 oz pink rolled fondant
* 4 oz blue rolled fondant
* Edible pearlized dusting powder
* Fine floristry wire
* Edible silver food coloring
* Confectioners' sugar, for dusting
* Makes 10

One: Put the candy in a polythene bag and lightly crush with a rolling pin. Dust a work surface with confectioners' sugar and roll out the ivory fondant. Cut out 10 rectangles, each 1½ x 1 inch. Brush with a dampened paintbrush and press pieces of candy into the fondant.

Two: Cut out 10 strips, each 2½ x ½ inch, and bend the ends into a ring. Transfer all the pieces to a baking tray lined with baking parchment and leave to harden for at least 2 hours. Wrap the trimmings in plastic wrap and set aside.

Three: Use a metal spatula to spread the cooled cupcakes with the frosting. Thinly roll out the pink fondant and cut out 10 discs using a 3½ inch round cutter. Place one on top of each cupcake.

Four: Shape tiny balls from the remaining ivory fondant and the blue fondant, rolling the ivory balls in pearl dusting powder. Thread rows of balls onto 3½-inch lengths of floristry wire and drape around the cakes, pushing the wire ends into the fondant to hold in place. Use a dampened paintbrush to secure more balls on the fondant.

Five: Paint the ring using silver food coloring, allow to dry, and secure on the tops of the cupcakes.

Luscious Lips

* 1 quantity Buttercream (see page 12) * 10 Tutti Fruiti Cupcakes (see page 10)
* 5 oz red rolled fondant * 1 tablespoon strawberry jelly * Confectioners' sugar, for dusting
* Makes 10

One: Spread the buttercream over the tops of the cooled cupcakes using a metal spatula.

Two: Take ½ oz of the red fondant, dust your hands with confectioners' sugar and mold the fondant into the shape of a pair of lips. Position on one of the cupcakes, then shape the remainder in the same way.

Three: Pass the strawberry jelly through a strainer to remove any lumps. Use a small paintbrush to brush the jelly over the lips to give a glossy sheen.

Feel the Heat

8 oz white-flavored semisweet chocolate, chopped ✻ 1 tablespoon (½ stick) unsalted butter ✻ 12 Chocolate Chile Cupcakes (see page 9) ✻ 13 oz red rolled fondant ✻ 2 oz white rolled fondant ✻ Black food coloring ✻ Confectioners' sugar, for dusting ✻ Makes 12

One: Melt the chocolate with the butter (see page 15). Once the chocolate has cooled and thickened slightly, but not set, spoon a little over the top of each cooled cupcake and use a metal spatula to smooth.

Two: Roll ¾ oz of red fondant into a ball and flatten until it is about 2 inches in diameter. Dust your fingers with confectioners' sugar and shape small pieces of white fondant to make a mouth and eyes. Position on the red fondant disc to make a face, securing with a dampened paintbrush.

Three: Roll very thin ropes of red fondant and position around the mouth and tops of the eyes. Shape and position horns and a nose. Position the face on one of the cakes, then use a little more red fondant to make a pointy tail to drape round the sides of the cupcake. Repeat with the remaining cakes.

Four: Use the black food coloring and a fine paintbrush to finish the eyes.

Caged

* 10 *Tutti Frutti Cupcakes (see page 10)* * 1 *quantity White Chocolate Ganache (see page 13)*
* 5 *oranges* * 3½ oz *clear hard candy* * 4 *tablespoons strawberry jelly* * 10 *fresh strawberries*
* *Vegetable oil, for brushing* * **Makes 10**

One: Preheat the oven to 400°F. Use a metal spatula to swirl the cooled cupcakes with the ganache. Brush the oranges with vegetable oil, wrap them tightly in plastic wrap, and place on a work surface with the plastic wrap ends underneath. Brush again lightly with vegetable oil.

Two: Make a small bowl out of a piece of aluminum foil, place on a baking tray, and unwrap half the candy into it. Put in the preheated oven for about 15 minutes or until the mints have melted and the syrup is bubbling.

Three: Working quickly, dip a fork into the candy syrup and drizzle it back and forth across the top half of an orange. Repeat the dipping and drizzling, criss-crossing until the orange is fairly thickly coated in fine lines of syrup. Repeat on the remaining oranges. If the syrup hardens before you've had time to coat all the oranges, return it to the oven to soften again.

Four: Leave the syrup until brittle, then carefully unravel the plastic wrap and pull out the oranges. Ease the plastic wrap away from the cages and transfer them to a lightly oiled sheet of foil. Make 5 more cages in the same way with the remaining candy.

Five: Press the strawberry jelly through a strainer to remove any lumps. Position a cage at a tilted angle on each cupcake and perch a strawberry inside. Drizzle with the jelly.

Luscious in Leather

12 Rich Chocolate Cupcakes (see page 9) ✱ 1 quantity Dark Chocolate Ganache (see page 13) ✱ 3 oz each of black, lilac, and deep pink rolled fondant ✱ Tube of black writing icing ✱ Silver dragees ✱ Confectioners' sugar, for dusting ✱ Makes 12

One: Use a metal spatula to spread the cooled cupcakes with the ganache, doming it up in the center and spreading it down as smoothly as possible.

Two: Dust a work surface with confectioners' sugar, thinly roll out the black fondant, and cut into thin strips about ½ inch wide. Arrange one piece on each cupcake to make a belt, trimming off the ends to fit. Make holes in the remaining black strips and lay on top of the belts at one end, securing them in place with a dampened paintbrush. Make more belts with the lilac and pink fondants.

Three: Use the writing icing to pipe buckles on some of the belts and the silver dragees to make buckles on the others, holding them in place with tiny blobs of writing icing.

Drive Me Wild

12 Chocolate Chile Cupcakes (see page 9) ✹ ½ quantity Vodka Buttercream (see page 12) ✹ 8 oz white rolled fondant ✹ Orange and brown food colorings ✹ 2 oz black rolled fondant ✹ 3 oz red rolled fondant ✹ Pink or red dusting powder (optional) ✹ Confectioners' sugar, for dusting ✹ Makes 12

One: Use a small metal spatula to spread the cooled cakes with the buttercream, doming it up in the centers.

Two: Color the white fondant with orange coloring (see page 14), adding a dash of brown if the orange is very bright. Now separate 2 oz of the orange fondant and work in some brown coloring to darken it. Wrap the two colors separately in plastic wrap and set aside.

Three: Dust a work surface with confectioners' sugar and roll out ½ of the orange fondant to form a 2½ inch disc. Break off tiny balls of the black fondant, flatten them slightly and press gently onto the orange disc, spacing them about ¼ inch apart. Press even smaller balls of brown fondant on top of the black fondant. Using a rolling pin, gently roll the fondant so the colors merge. Cut out a disc using a 3½ inch round cutter and position over one of the cupcakes, tucking the fondant in around the edges. Repeat with the remaining cakes.

Four: Shape the red icing into little handbags, add a black clasp to each and secure on the tops of the cupcakes with a dampened paintbrush. Finish by dusting the handbags with the dusting powder, if liked.

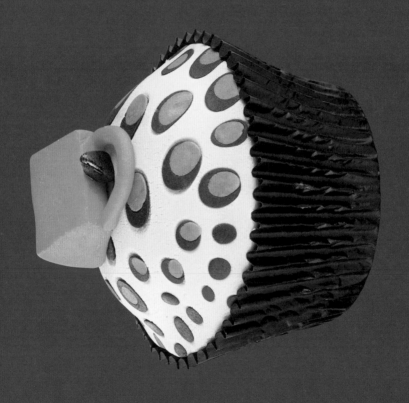

Peek~a~boo!

10 Red Velvet Cupcakes (see page 11) ✹ ½ quantity Vodka Buttercream (see page 12) ✹ 13 oz flesh-colored rolled fondant ✹ Scant 2 cups royal icing sugar ✹ Dark blue and edible gold food colorings ✹ Piping sparkles (optional) ✹ Confectioners' sugar, for dusting ✹ Makes 10

One: Use a metal spatula to spread the cooled cupcakes with the buttercream.

Two: Dust your hands with confectioners' sugar, take a ¾ oz ball of flesh-colored fondant, and cut in half. Flatten each half slightly into a breast shape and position on one of the cakes. Repeat with the remainder.

Three: Dust a work surface with confectioners' sugar and thinly roll out the remaining icing. Cut out 10 discs using an 3½ inch round cutter. Lay then over the cupcakes, smoothing to fit and eliminating any creases.

Four: Beat the royal icing sugar in a bowl with 5–6 teaspoons of water to make a smooth icing that only just holds its shape. Set aside one-third of the icing in a separate bowl and color the remainder dark blue. Spoon the blue icing into a paper piping bag (see page 10) fitted with a decorating tip and use to pipe lacy bra designs onto the breasts.

Five: Put the reserved white royal icing in another piping bag fitted with a decorating tip and pipe little flower and a necklace. Leave the icing to set before painting the necklace and flower with gold food coloring. Pipe a dot of piping sparkles in the middle of each necklace, if liked.

Strangers in the Night

Generous 1¹⁄₂ cups royal icing sugar ❋ Deep red food coloring ❋ 10 Red Velvet Cupcakes (see page 11) ❋ 1 quantity Vodka Buttercream (see page 12) ❋ 8 oz orange rolled fondant ❋ 2 oz black rolled fondant ❋ Tube of black writing icing ❋ Confectioners' sugar, for dusting ❋ Makes 10

One: Trace the outline of a mask onto a piece of baking parchment. It should be roughly 3½ inches across. For guidance use the photograph opposite, or refer to a book or the Internet to source your image.

Two: Put the royal icing sugar in a bowl and add enough water, about 5 teaspoons, to mix to a smooth paste. Beat in the red food coloring. Put a third of the icing in a paper piping bag (see page 14) and snip off the merest tip.

Three: Place another sheet of parchment over the outline. Pipe icing around the shape, then pipe another wavy edge round the outside. Slide the top sheet of parchment along so you can pipe more masks. Add a few drops of water to the remaining icing, put in another piping bag with a larger hole, and fill in the centers of the masks. Leave to harden overnight.

Four: Spread the cooled cupcakes with buttercream. Dust a work surface with confectioners' sugar, roll out the orange fondant and cut 10 discs using a 3½-inch round cutter. Position a disc on each cake, then secure the masks in place with a dampened paintbrush. Roll out the black fondant. Cut into strips, then attach one to each cake. Finish by using the black writing icing to pipe a border round each mask.

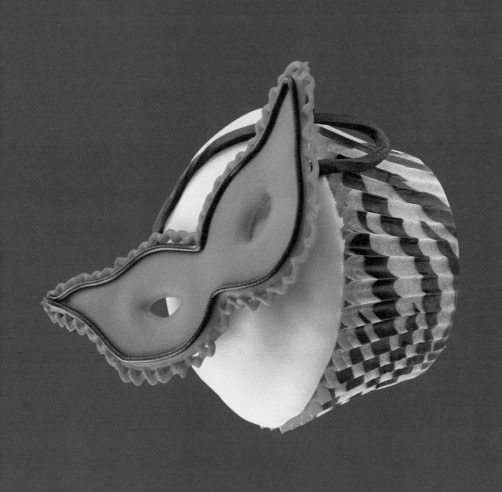

Sex Kitten

1 quantity *Vanilla Buttercream* (see page 12) * 10 *Vanilla Cupcakes* (see page 8)
* 8 oz *white rolled fondant* * *Pink and black food colorings* * 4 oz *black rolled fondant*
* 2 oz *deep pink rolled fondant* * *Edible gold food coloring* * *Confectioners' sugar, for dusting*
* Makes 10

One: Use a metal spatula to spread the buttercream over the tops of the cooled cupcakes.

Two: Dust a work surface with confectioners' sugar, roll out the white fondant thinly and cut out 10 discs using a 3½ inch round cutter. Position a disc on each cupcake and smooth gently. Gather up the trimmings and knead in a little pink food coloring to make a pale pink icing. Wrap in plastic wrap and set aside.

Three: Thinly roll out the black fondant and cut out a 3½ inch disc. Press the cutter into the disc again to create a crescent. Secure on one of the cakes using a dampened paintbrush. Repeat with the remaining cakes, rerolling the trimmings to make more crescents. Use more of the black fondant to make ears and position on the cakes. Reserve the trimmings.

Four: Thinly roll out the deep pink fondant and use the round cutter and a knife to shape the hair. Use the trimmings to shape lips.

Five: Use the pale pink fondant to make the centers of the ears, the noses, and collars. Use a fine paintbrush and black food coloring to paint eyes and whiskers. Thinly roll the reserved black fondant and cut out long, thick eyelashes. Secure in place using a dampened paintbrush, then finish by painting gold spots on the collars.

Love Bites

* 10 Red Velvet Cupcakes (see page 11) * ½ quantity Cream Cheese Frosting (see page 12)
* 8 oz burgundy rolled fondant * 10 oz black rolled fondant
* Tube of brown writing icing * Black food coloring * 4 oz white rolled fondant
* Confectioners' sugar, for dusting * Makes 10

One: Use a metal spatula to spread the cream cheese frosting on the cooled cupcakes. Dust a work surface with confectioners' sugar, thinly roll out the burgundy fondant, and cut out 10 discs using a 3½ inch round cutter. Position on the cakes. Reserve the trimmings.

Two: Reserve 1 oz of black fondant for the collars and divide the remainder into 10 pieces. Roll out one piece into a 8 inch strip, 1¾ inches wide at one end tapering to ⅞ inch at the other. Dampen the edge of a cake with a paintbrush and wrap the strip around it, tucking the narrower end behind the wide end. Repeat with the remainder. Thinly roll out the black fondant trimmings, cut out 10 bats, and add balls of burgundy fondant for eyes.

Three: Work a small piece of burgundy fondant into the white fondant to make it pink. Roll into balls for heads and press into position, then make 10 hands and secure behind the cloaks. Thinly roll out the reserved black and burgundy fondants, place one on top of the other and gently reroll. Cut into 1¼ inch wide strips and then into rectangles with the long side about 2½ inches. Secure behind the heads for collars.

Four: Scribble brown writing icing onto the heads for hair and use a fine paintbrush and black food coloring to paint features on the faces. Shape tiny pieces of red fondant into drips of blood and use a dampened paintbrush to secure them to the cloaks. Gently press the bats onto the sides of the cakes. If they don't stick, use a little of the frosting to secure them.

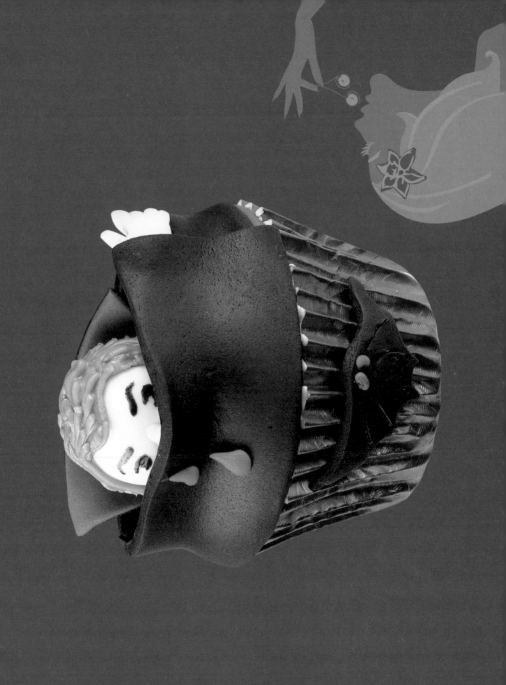

Cupid's Revenge

1 oz deep red rolled fondant ❋ 3 cups confectioners' sugar, plus extra for dusting ❋ 3~4 tablespoons lemon juice ❋ Black food coloring ❋ 10 Red Velvet Cupcakes (see page 11) ❋ Makes 10

One: Dust a work surface with confectioners' sugar and thickly roll out the red fondant. Cut out 10 hearts using a 1½-inch cutter. Use the tip of a sharp knife to cut off about one-third of each heart in a jagged line. Push a piece of wooden cocktail stick up through the middle of each piece of heart from the base. Transfer all the pieces to a baking tray lined with baking parchment and leave for at least 2 hours to harden. Wrap the fondant trimmings in plastic wrap and set aside.

Two: Beat the confectioners' sugar in a bowl with enough lemon juice to make an icing that thickly covers the back of a spoon. Transfer one-third of the icing to a separate bowl and color it dark grey using black food coloring.

Three: Spread the white icing over the cooled cupcakes, allowing it to drizzle down the sides. If it is too thick to drizzle, add a drop more lemon juice. If it is too runny, beat in a little more confectioners' sugar. Drizzle the grey icing over the white.

Four: While the icing is still wet, shape the red fondant trimmings into small teardrops and push gently into the icing at the front and down the sides of the cupcakes. Secure the heart pieces to the cupcakes by pushing the cocktail sticks down into the cakes.

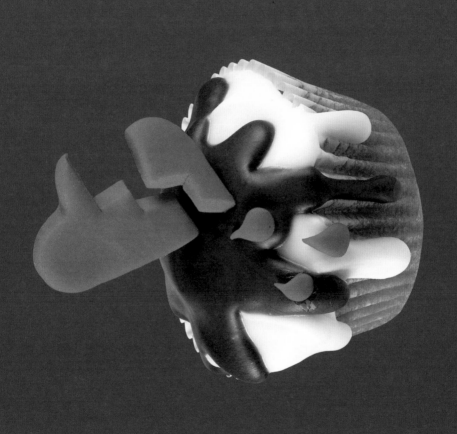

Baby Doll

12 Rich Chocolate Cupcakes (see page 9) ✻ ½ quantity Dark Chocolate Ganache (see page 13) ✻ 1 lb. white almond paste ✻ Pink food coloring ✻ Generous 2 cups royal icing sugar ✻ 3 oz black rolled fondant ✻ Confectioners' sugar, for dusting ✻ Makes 12

One: Use a metal spatula to spread the cupcakes with the ganache. Take a piece of almond paste the size of a walnut and cut in half. Shape into two balls, flatten slightly and press into the ganache ½ inch apart near one edge of a cake. Repeat with the other cakes.

Two: Dust a work surface with confectioners' sugar and knead a little pink food coloring into the remaining almond paste. Roll out thinly and cut out 12 discs using a 3½ inch round cutter. Cut off a ½ inch strip from the two opposite sides of the discs to give straight sides. Lay over the cupcakes, smoothing around the breasts. Use a fine paintbrush and a little food coloring to paint nipples.

Three: Put the royal icing sugar in a bowl and add enough water, about 6–7 teaspoons, to mix to a smooth paste. Put two-thirds in a paper piping bag (see page 14) fitted with a fine decorating tip. Use to pipe lacy baby doll nighties over the cupcakes.

Four: Roll out the black fondant thinly, cut into ½ inch wide strips and ruffle the strips (see page 15). Position on the nighties so the ruffles overhang the edges of the cupcakes. Color the remaining piping icing pink and put in another piping bag. Use to pipe the decorative bow.

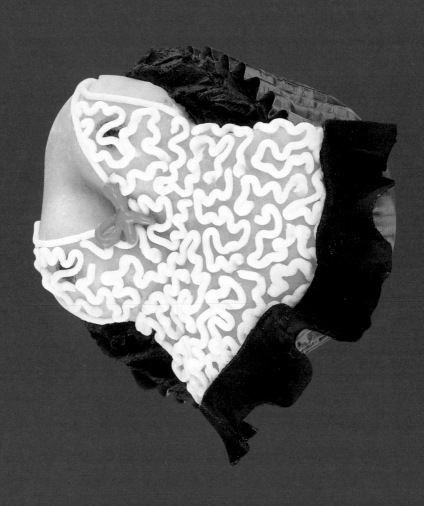

Love Birds

Generous 1½ cups royal icing sugar ✻ Ivory and navy blue food colorings ✻ 10 Exotic Spice Cupcakes (see page 10) ✻ ½ quantity Buttercream (see page 12) ✻ 2½ cups confectioners sugar ✻ Makes 10

One: Trace the outlines of 2 love birds onto a piece of baking parchment. They should be roughly 2 inches from beak to tail. For guidance use the photograph opposite, or refer to a book or the Internet to source your image.

Two: Put the royal icing sugar in a large bowl and add enough water, about 5–6 teaspoons, to mix to a smooth paste. Beat in a few drops of ivory food coloring.

Three: Put a third of the icing in a paper piping bag (see page 14) and snip off the merest tip. Place another sheet of parchment over the bird outlines. Pipe icing around the edges of the shapes, then slide the top sheet of parchment along so you can pipe more birds. Use the remaining icing in the bag to pipe some hearts.

Four: Add a few drops of water to the remaining icing, put in another piping bag with a larger hole and fill in the centers of the birds and hearts. Leave to harden overnight.

Five: Use a metal spatula to spread the cooled cupcakes with the buttercream. Put the confectioners' sugar in a bowl and add about 2–3 tablespoons water, or enough to make a smooth icing that coats the back of the spoon. Beat in navy blue food coloring and spread over the cupcakes, allowing to drip over the sides a little. Position the birds and hearts on the cupcakes, securing the hearts with icing and propping up the birds with cocktail sticks, if necessary.

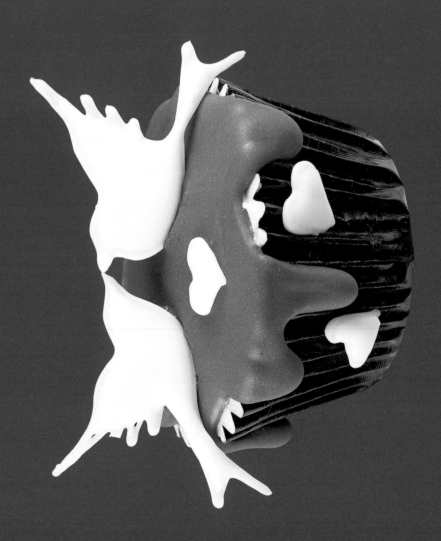

Eastern Promise

10 oz semisweet chocolate, chopped ✻ 12 Chocolate Rose Cupcakes (see page 9)
✻ 1 lb rose-flavored Turkish delight, chopped ✻ Silver dragees ✻ Makes 12

One: Melt the chocolate (see page 15) and spread a teaspoonful over the top of each cooled cupcake.

Two: Pile lots of chopped Turkish delight on top of each cake.

Three: Use a teaspoon to drizzle chocolate over the tops of the cakes so it falls over and between the Turkish delight, without completely coating it. Finish the cupcakes with silver dragees. These cakes are best served on the day they're decorated.

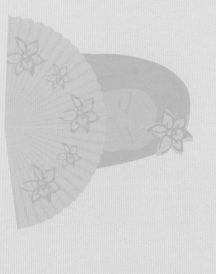

French Fancy

Scant 2 cups royal icing sugar ✻ Black food coloring ✻ 10 Tutti Frutti Cupcakes (see page 10)
✻ ½ quantity Buttercream (see page 12) ✻ 4 oz each of dark blue, turquoise, and deep pink rolled
fondant ✻ Confectioners' sugar, for dusting ✻ Makes 10

One: Trace the outline of a pair of kicking legs, roughly 3½ inches long, onto a piece of baking parchment. For guidance use the picture opposite, or refer to a book or the Internet to source your image.

Two: Put the royal icing sugar in a bowl and add enough water, about 6 teaspoons, to mix to a smooth paste. Beat in the black food coloring. Put a third of the icing in a paper piping bag (see page 14) and snip off the merest tip.

Three: Place another sheet of parchment over the outline. Pipe icing around the shape, then slide the top sheet of parchment along so you can pipe more legs. Add a few drops of water to the remaining icing, put in another piping bag with a larger hole, and fill in the centers of the shapes. Leave to harden overnight.

Four: Use a metal spatula to spread the cooled cupcakes with the buttercream. Dust a work surface with confectioners' sugar and roll out some of the blue rolled fondant into a strip about ¾ inch wide. Ruffle one edge of the strip (see page 15). Lay the ruffled strips around the edges of the cupcakes.

Five: Use the pink and turquoise fondants to shape more ruffles and arrange on the cakes as shown. Use turquoise fondant to make garters, securing with a dampened paintbrush. Make a slit in the center of each cupcake with a knife and press the legs into position.

Cheek to Cheek

10 Tutti-Frutti Cupcakes (see page 10) * ½ quantity Buttercream (see page 12) * 1 lb flesh-colored rolled fondant * 3½ oz black rolled fondant * Generous 2 cups royal icing sugar * Black food coloring * Confectioners' sugar, for dusting * Makes 10

One: Use a metal spatula to spread the cooled cupcakes with the buttercream.

Two: Dust your hands with confectioners' sugar. Take a 1 oz ball of flesh-colored fondant and cut it in half. Flatten each half slightly and position on one of the cakes to form a bottom shape. Repeat with the remainder.

Three: Dust a work surface with confectioners' sugar and thinly roll out the remaining fondant. Cut out 10 discs using a 3½ inch round cutter. Lay them over the cakes, smoothing to fit and eliminating any creases. Use a sharp knife to make a cut between the cheeks.

Four: Thinly roll out the black fondant and cut out 10 skimpy bikinis. Gently press onto the cupcakes, securing in place with a dampened paintbrush and trimming off any excess at the sides.

Five: Beat the royal icing sugar in a bowl with 5–6 teaspoons of water to make a smooth icing that only just holds its shape. Set aside one-quarter of the icing in a separate bowl and color the remainder black. Spoon into a paper piping bag (see page 14) fitted with a fine decorating tip and use to pipe suspenders and stocking tops onto the cupcakes.

Six: Put the reserved white icing in another piping bag fitted with a fine decorating tip and pipe white lines along the suspenders and little flowers to finish.

Hey Suspender!

Generous 2 cups royal icing sugar ✳ Pink, black, and red food colorings ✳ 1 quantity White Chocolate Ganache (see page 13) ✳ 10 Vanilla Cupcakes (see page 8) ✳ Makes 10

One: Trace the outline of a pair of legs with high heeled shoes onto a piece of baking parchment. They should be roughly 3 inches long. For guidance use the photograph opposite, or refer to a book or the Internet to source your image.

Two: Put the royal icing sugar in a bowl and add enough water, about 6 teaspoons, to mix to a smooth paste. Beat in a dash of pink food coloring. Put a third of the icing in a paper piping bag (see page 14) and snip off the merest tip.

Three: Place another sheet of parchment over the outline. Pipe icing around the shape, then slide the top sheet of parchment along so you can pipe more legs. Add a few drops of water to the remaining icing, put in another piping bag with a larger hole, and fill in the centers of the shapes. Leave to harden overnight.

Four: Place the chocolate ganache in a large paper piping bag fitted with a star-shaped decorating tip and pipe swirls on the cupcakes.

Five: Use black and red food colorings and a fine paintbrush to paint suspenders, stockings, and shoes onto the icing legs. Leave to dry, then press a pair of legs into the top of each cupcake.

Bunny Girl

1 quantity *Antonetta Buttercream* (see page 12) ✳ 10 *Cherry Cupcakes* (see page 8)
✳ *Generous 2 cups royal icing sugar* ✳ *Black food coloring* ✳ *3½ oz pink rolled fondant*
✳ *7 oz black rolled fondant* ✳ *1 oz white rolled fondant* ✳ *Confectioners' sugar, for dusting*
✳ Makes 10

One: Use a metal spatula to spread buttercream smoothly on the cupcakes.

Two: Beat the royal icing sugar in a bowl with enough water, about 6 teaspoons, to make an icing that just holds its shape. Color with black food coloring and put in a paper piping bag (see page 14), fitted with a fine decorating tip. Alternatively, put in a paper piping bag and snip off the merest tip.

Three: Pipe parallel lines, about ¼ inch apart, over the cupcakes, then across in the opposite direction to give a "fishnet" design. Reserve the remaining icing.

Four: Dust a work surface with confectioners' sugar, roll out the pink fondant and cut out lots of small bow ties. Secure around the edges of the cakes. You'll need 8–10 per cupcake.

Five: Cut the black fondant into 10 equal pieces, dust your hands with confectioners' sugar, and mold each into a bunny costume. Insert a cocktail stick into the base of each and use to stick them on the cupcakes. Roll the white fondant into 10 pea-sized balls and position one on each costume for a tail, securing in place with a dampened paintbrush. Use the remaining black piping icing to create the lacing down the backs of the bunny costumes.

Minky Boots

Generous 2 cups royal icing sugar ✳ Purple and black food colorings ✳ 10 Vanilla Cupcakes (see page 8) ✳ 1 quantity White Chocolate Ganache (see page 13) ✳ Makes 10

One: Trace the outline of a pair of thigh-high boots onto a piece of baking parchment. They should be roughly 3 inches long. For guidance use the photograph opposite, or refer to a book or the Internet to source your image.

Two: Put the royal icing sugar in a bowl and add enough water, about 6 teaspoons, to mix to a smooth paste. Reserve 3 tablespoons of the icing in a separate bowl and cover tightly. Beat purple food coloring into the remainder. Put one-third of the purple icing in a paper piping bag (see page 14) and snip off the merest tip.

Three: Place another sheet of parchment over the boot outlines. Pipe icing around the edges of the shapes, then slide the top sheet of parchment along so you can pipe more boots. Add a few drops of water to the remaining purple icing, put in another piping bag with a larger hole, and fill in the centers of the boots. Leave to harden overnight.

Four: Use a metal spatula to spread the cooled cupcakes with the ganache. Gently press a pair of boots onto the ganache, supporting them at the back with a cocktail stick, if necessary. Color the remaining icing black and put in another piping bag, snipping off the merest tip. Use to decorate the boots and the edges of the cupcakes with tassels.

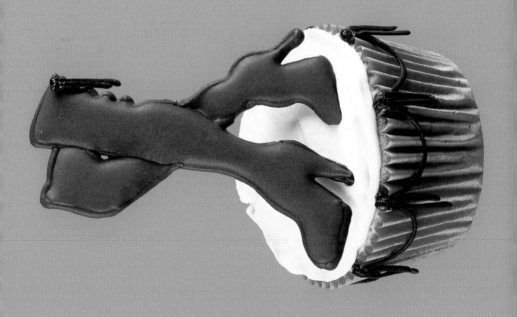

Down Boy

10 oz black rolled fondant ❋ 12 Rich Chocolate Cupcakes (see page 9) ❋ ½ quantity Dark Chocolate Ganache (see page 13) ❋ 7 oz brown rolled fondant ❋ 3½ oz red rolled fondant ❋ 20 ft wired ribbon ❋ Confectioners' sugar, for dusting ❋ Makes 12

One: Dust your hands with confectioners' sugar and shape ½ oz of black fondant into a drum shape for a hat, then ¼ oz into a disc for the brim. Secure together with a dampened paintbrush and transfer to a baking tray lined with baking parchment. Make 11 more in the same way.

Two: Roll a little more black fondant into a rope about ⅛ inch wide, and cut into 1½ inch lengths for the whip handles. Transfer to the baking tray and leave for several hours to harden. Wrap and reserve the remaining black fondant.

Three: Use a metal spatula to spread the cooled cupcakes with ganache. Dust a work surface with confectioners' sugar and roll out the brown fondant thinly. Roll the red fondant into very thin ropes, then lay them over the brown fondant, spaced ½ inch apart. Gently roll with the rolling pin to make stripes. Cut out 12 discs using a 3½ inch round cutter and lay over the cakes.

Four: Cut the ribbon into 12 lengths and tie around the cupcakes. Position the hats and whip handles on the cupcakes, securing with a dampened paintbrush. Roll the reserved black fondant as thinly as possible under your fingers and arrange over the cupcakes in loops to make the whips.

Acknowledgments

Publisher: Sarah Ford
Managing Editor: Camilla Davis
Designer: Joanna MacGregor
Illustrator: Vanessa Bell
Food Stylist: Joanna Farrow
Photographer: Edward Allwright

Many of the cupcake cases were kindly supplied by *Kalasform* who specialize in decorative paper cupcake cases. Check out their website www.kalasform.se or look out for their products in specialist cake decorating stores or through internet mail order companies.